Zoé Unakim

Aufstieg

Zoé Unakim

Aufstieg

in die fünfte Dimension

Trainerverlag

Imprint

Cover image: www.ingimage.com

Publisher:
Der Trainerverlag
is a trademark of
International Book Market Service Ltd., member of OmniScriptum Publishing Group
17 Meldrum Street, Beau Bassin 71504, Mauritius
Printed at: see last page
ISBN: 978-620-0-76907-7

Inhaltsverzeichnis:

I. <u>Penta Dimension:</u>

„*<u>-Achtung:</u> Hier habe ich ein sehr interessantes Video! [...] super tolle Aussagen! Die ganze Welt in 10 Minuten!*“[1]

„Fick die Lügen – wen wollt ihr hier verarschen?

Und für eure Lügen soll ich dann noch GEZ bezahlen?

Egal ob Tagesschau, Bundestag oder schon im Kindergarten

Alles Lüge! Bestenfalls wissen sie nicht was sie da sagen

In der Schule lernst du gar nix außer wie du Sklave brav bist

Dass du nachsitzt wennst nicht nachgibst, Kreativität fürn Arsch ist

Dass du weiterkommst wenn du wiederholst was gar nicht wahr ist

Sie verstehen nur spanisch viele komm nicht klar & werden panisch

Aber so ist das System, also Sklave hinterfrag nicht

An der Uni auf der Arbeit kriegen wir die selbe Nachricht

Gib bei Google mal wie Worte „Schule macht mich“ ein & frag dich

Was da falsch läuft es ist tragisch, Mobbinganzahl steigt dramatisch

---

[1] Vgl. https://www.geistheiler-sananda.net/blog-aktuell/

Das ist kein Zufall, Nein das ganze hat System

Sie wollen nicht dass wir verstehen um was es eigentlich hier geht

Unsere Zirbeldrüse ist verkalkt doch keinen interessiert´s

Weil keiner weiß was eine Zirbeldrüse ist, was sie bewirkt

Wir wurden programmiert

Du denkst wirklich dass es deine Meinung wäre

Doch du rennst nur einer Herde hinterher wie ein paar Pferde

Aufwachen ist so schwer dank kognitiver Dissonanz

Keiner will besonders sein, gleichgeschaltet, Gruppenzwang

Die Lügen gehen weit zurück, zig Generationen

Und die Wahrheit wird so streng gehütet in geheimen Logen

Sie wissen dass sie lügen und sie steuern uns wie Züge

Die Agenda bleibt die gleiche egal ob Merkel oder Grüne

Das ganze Geldsystem dient nur einem Zweck

Und zwar dass die Ungerechtigkeit immer weiter wächst

Der Zinseszins und die Geldschöpfung dienen den Eliten

Das Volk muss schaffen dass die Reichen ihre Zinsen kriegen

Energie ist frei! Und das wissen wir seit Tesla

Doch J.P. Morgan fand ein paar Milliarden Dollar besser

Genauso Nahrung: es gibt genug für jeden Mensch

Aber es wird lieber weg geschmissen als verschenkt

Jede Verschwörungstheorie wird zur Praxis

Wenn man sie ernst studiert sieht man dass das meiste Fakt ist

Unsere Erde wird regiert von Menschen die Satan dienen

Du kannst das nicht nachvollziehen

Doch weißt nichts von den schwarzen Riten

Treffen jedes Jahr im Bohemian Grove

Spielen Menschenopfer, die höchste Elite ist dort

Beten einen 15 Meter großen Moloch an in Kutten

Bringen ihm ein Menschenopfer – auch wenn nur als Puppe

Sei gewiss dass das nicht der letzte Vorhang ist der fallen wird

Schwarze Messen, Menschenopfer, rate mal was das bewirkt

Wikileaks hat es bewiesen: #Pizzagate ist wahr

Sie verschieben / quälen Kinder opfern sie auf dem Altar

Emails in denen sie schreiben wie alt die kids sind die zu einem

In den whirlpool steigen

Was zum Teufel soll das anderes heißen?

Soll ich Domino denn lieber über Käse als auf Pasta spielen?

Das sind Codes von Pädophilen

Wer das verneint gehört zu ihnen

Podesta child molester, Besta Pizza: check das Logo

Von dem Sprecher Dennis Hastert Sexverbrecher bis zum POTUS

#Killroom oder Folter, Kindersärge auf den Fotos

Wir zählen 1 und 1 zusammen

Denkt ihr wirklich wir sind so doof??

Joe Biden beim vereidigen hat nur Interesse an den Kleinen

Jeffrey Epstein fliegt mit Bill Clinton auf Lolita island

Alle die das noch verneinen und verschweigen haben eine

Mitverantwortung an einem Schwerverbrechen ohne Gleichen

Keine Untersuchungen, nur mediale Kampfansagen

An alle die es wagen Fragwürdiges zu hinterfragen

Du kannst es nicht glauben, dass diese Teufel Kinder foltern

Dann mach mal dein Fernseher aus und recherchiere MK Ultra

Folter unter Todesangst damit sich die Persönlichkeit

Der Kinder spaltet dafür muss man weitaus mehr als böse sein

Satanisten regieren diesen Planeten

Du glaubst das nicht? Bruder siehst du nicht wie wir hier leben?

Schau dir das Fern[s]ehen an, hör doch der Musik zu

Schau was für games wir zocken, was halten wir für cool?

Über was lachen wir? Schau was uns wichtig ist

Es geht um Geld und Macht, wenn das nicht Satanismus ist!

Doch das alles soll als normal gesehen werden

Die wenigsten hier wissen was sie tun bevor sie sterben

Schön blind, ignorant verbringen sie ihr Sklavenleben

Ohne zu wissen wem sie ihre Energie letztendlich geben

Sie vergiften unser Essen mit GMO und Pestiziden

Böden werden totgedüngt, wo sind all die Fliegen??

75% weniger Insekten!!!!!!!!!!!

Wie soll ich da glauben das Bundesumweltamt … will diese retten?

Sie vergiften unsre Luft, schau doch mal nach oben

Plötzlich gibt es neue Wolkenarten – bunt wie Regenbogen

Ich nahm Regenwasserproben: Gifte drin in hohen Dosen!

Egal wie man es nennt – das[s] da nichts drin ist ist gelogen!

Sie vergiften unsren Geist mit Lügen und Ängsten

Vergiften die Gemeinschaft durch betrügen und Grenzen

Vergiften unsre Erde mit Atommüll und Dünger

Vergiften unsren IQ denn die Menschen werden dümmer

Die Fruchtbarkeit geht drastisch zurück!

Doch als ob es scheissegal wäre macht sich keiner verrückt

So ein Zufall oder Glück aber das ist was sie wollen

Das erleichtert die Kontrolle die sie fordern Stück für Stück

Sie vergiften unsre Spiritualität

Die meisten lachen wenn man sie erwähnt als ob es sie nicht gäb

Sie wollen dass wir glauben dass Gott strafend und streng ist

Der einen in die Hölle schickt, die Erde ein Gefängnis

Soviele checken das sind keine Christen sondern Satanisten

Merken dass sie uns anlügen und werden dann zu Atheisten

Musst es selbst ausprobieren und aktiv erforschen

Glaub weder denen ... noch meinen Worten

Punkt 1: Alles was man dir gesagt hat ist gelogen

Über Terror oder Klima, Impfungen und Drogen

Von Kriegen, Physik, Erdgeschichte oder Krebs

In Unis, Kirchen, Fernsehen, ihr Geld ist der Weg

Punkt 2: Das alles machen sie nur weil sie Angst haben

Vor unserer Kraft und unserer Macht sobald wir das erkannt haben

Das kollektive Aufwachen müssen sie verhindern

Also halten sie uns dumm und vergiften unsere Kinder

Punkt 3: wir sind nicht begrenzt auf unseren Körper

Oder unsere 5 Sinne das sind Lügen dieser Mörder

Punkt 4: also haben wir einen Effekt

Auf feinstofflicher Ebene auf alles was hier wächst

Dankbarkeit und Liebe sind höhere Frequenzen

Als Hass und Ängste dementsprechend sind die Konsequenzen

Woher wissen was wahr ist? Denn wir kennen nur die Matrix

Wir haben vergessen wer wir sind, sind Wesen ohne Basis

Punkt 5: und das ist der beste aller Punkte

Nullpunktenergie heißt ein Lichtjahr pro Sekunde

Sowohl Raum als auch Raumzeit ist eine Illusion

Wir haben das Wissen + die Technik frag das Team um TomDeLonge

Um es nochmal zu betonen: UFOs sind real!

Du hast mich schon verstanden ich wiederhole es gleich nochmal

Ja, UFOs sind real! Und waren es schon immer

Doch globale Einmischung macht alles nur noch schlimmer

Sie sahen dass wir unsere Erde atomar verwüsten

Wollten uns bewahren vor unseren Taten und atomaren Wüsten

Sie haben nicht nur Technik die unserer weit voraus ist

Sondern sind spirituell so weit voraus du glaubst es nicht

Das macht es kompliziert wie soll man da kommunizieren

Sie haben einen Plan den die meisten lang noch nicht kapieren

Und dieser Plan hat mit Reinkarnation zu tun

Seelen von anderen Planeten sind hier um nun

Unsere Frequenzen auf dem Planeten hier anzuheben

Damit niedrige Frequenzen es nicht schaffen zu bestehen

Diese müssen dadurch gehen und woanders weiterleben

Damit Gaia endlich aufsteigen kann mit ihren Wesen

Und diese Lebewesen von fremden Planeten werden

Observiert und untersucht oft ohne es zu merken

Sowohl körperlich als auch auf Seelenebene drauf vorbereitet

Dass sie funken wenn die Erde high wird wie durch Schoresteine

Funken wie bei Morsezeichen, lange wird es nicht mehr dauern

Unsere Sonne hat nämlich jetzt jede Woche mehr an Power

Meinetwegen werd jetzt sauer oder fang zu grinsen an

Dann merkst du mal körperlich die kognitive Dissonanz

Aber wenn du wissen willst ob ich meine Hausaufgaben

Gut gemacht hab in den letzten 1000 Tagen / 1000 Fragen

Schau nach Namen wie Prof. John Mack oder Dr. Leir

Die Beweise waren gut verschwiegen aber immer hier

#Disclosure Project – hunderte von Militärs

Haben eidesstattlich und faktisch alles erklärt

Doch dann kam der 11.9. alle senden nur noch davon

Es wäre fast passiert, doch der mediale Kanon

Verschweigt die Zeugen, die Ereignisse und die Beweise

Selbst wenn alles Lügen wären: Warum waren alle leise?

Hätte es dich interessiert, sag hättest du sie hören wollen?

Wenn Militärpiloten ihre UFO-Jagd beschwören sollen?

Dokumente zeigen dass sie absolut die Wahrheit sagen

Radardaten von UFOs über Nuklearanlagen

Chefpiloten ... Astronauten ...

Ich glaub du wirst es nicht glauben

Wenn du selber siehst was für Menschen all das so behaupten

Jetzt liegt´s an dir was du aus der Info machen wirst

Du kannst meinetwegen glauben für was die Elite wirbt

Du kannst glauben dass du stirbst, dass Feuer den Einsturz bewirkt

Dann aber hast du deine Chance auf eine neue Welt verwirkt.

Dann musst du weiterziehen an irgendeinen anderen Ort

Wo es für dich weiter geht mit Elend, Hunger, Terror, Mord

Ich und andere leben dann hier weiter ohne Tiere schlachten

Ohne die Vergiftungen, die Lügen oder Krieg und Schlachten

Alles kein Problem, wie anfangs schon gesagt:

Keiner urteilt über dich! Jeder so wie er es mag

Aber Gaia hat genug und will jetzt endlich mal auch in die schon

Lange überfällige 5. Dimension“[2]

„Penta Dimension … In die Fünfte Dimension (Da hat aber mal jemand so richtig seine Hausaufgaben gemacht … alles drin … HARTER TOBAK!!!)“[3]

---

[2] Vgl. https://www.youtube.com/watch?v=x1rzuBp8Rbw&feature=youtu.be

[3] Vgl. https://www.esistallesda.de/2020/11/10/penta-dimension-in-die-fuenfte-dimension-da-hat- aber-mal-jemand-so-richtig-seine-hausaufgaben-gemacht-alles-drin-harter-tobak/

II. DIE FÜNFTE DIMENSION:[4]

Gibt es 'nen Gott,
oder gibt es keinen?
Ist die Hölle schon voll,

oder pass ich noch rein?

Werd' ich geliebt,
oder bin ich alleine?
Und kann man völlig außer sich
doch eigentlich so insgeheim ganz bei sich sein?

Bin ich gut,
oder bin ich böse?
Bin ich Teil der Lösung
oder das Problem?

Bin ich verbohrt,
oder zeige ich Größe?
Und warum soll ich eigentlich
immer dann, wenn es am Schönsten ist, nach Hause geh'n?

Die Fragerei geht hier und jetzt zu Ende.
Hier kommt die kosmische Botschaft aus der fünften Dimension.
Aus der fünften Dimension.

---

[4] Vgl. https://www.songtexte.com/songtext/wirtz/die-funfte-dimension-g3e40113.html

Wir führen euch auf völlig neues Gelände.
Wir schießen euch in den reatonalen Orion.
Reatonalen Orion.

Weiß man zu lieben,
oder muss man es lernen?
Hat unser Leben einen tieferen Sinn?

Was genau steht eigentlich in den Sternen?
Wer hat's geschrieben?
Und wie zur Hölle kam der überhaupt da hin?

Die Fragerei geht hier und jetzt zu Ende.
Hier kommt der kosmische Bote aus der fünften Dimension.
Aus der fünften Dimension.

Ich führe euch durch völlig neues Gelände.
Ich inizier' euch das reatonale Glückshormon.
Reatonale Glückshormon.

Is' es denn nun wichtig,
oder ist es scheiß egal?
Is' es denn so richtig,
oder falsch in diesem Fall?

Muss ich denn nun wirklich über sieben Brücken geh'n?
Und wenn ja, wer kann mir sagen, wo diese scheiß Brücken steh'n?

Hab ich den Durchblick
oder keine Ahnung?
Bin ich abgestumpft
oder tut es noch weh?

Fehlt mir das Zeug
oder nur die Erfahrung?
Und warum wechselt der Rasen
seine Farbe, wenn ich auf der and'ren Seite steh'?

Ja, ihr könnt den Wald vor lauter Bäumen
schon lange nicht mehr seh'n.
Dass ist das Problem!

Und darum ist jetzt Schluss
mit dieser kleinkarierten Dreidimensionalität.
Bitte gern' gescheh'n!

Die Fragerei geht hier und jetzt zu Ende.
Hier kommt die kosmische Botschaft aus der fünften Dimension.
Aus der fünften Dimension.

Wir führen euch auf völlig neues Gelände.
Wir schießen euch in den reatonalen Orion.
Reatonalen Orion.

Die Fragerei geht hier und jetzt zu Ende.
Hier kommt der kosmische Bote aus der fünften Dimension.

Aus der fünften Dimension.

Ich führe euch durch völlig neues Gelände.
Ich inizier' euch das reatonale Glückshormon.
reatonale Glückshormon.

III. Fünfte Dimension:[5]

Gestern - Herzfrequenzen noch normal
Heute - umgibt mich ein Gerüst aus Stahl
Was wichtig war, ist reduziert auf null

Herzton - von Maschinen abgehört
Computer - von eignen Daten ganz verwirrt
Die Wissenschaft, die Technik hat keine Chance

Strahlen - wirre Klänge häufen sich
Strahlen - die Erinnerung erlischt
Ich fühl Energie und ich beginn zu

Schweben in das Licht
Kein Atemzug und kein Gefühl
Ich fliege ohne mich
Hoch, tief, Raum und Zeit
Kein Anfang und kein Ende
Und auch keine Wirklichkeit
Reinkarnation
In Lichtgeschwindigkeit als heller
Strahlenstrom zur fünften Dimension

Körper - degradiert zu Material
Wärme - entzieh ich ihm mit einem Mal
Ich fühl Energie und ich beginn zu

Schweben in das Licht

---

[5] Vgl. https://www.karaoke-texte.de/liedtexte/schilling-peter/funfte-dimension-934490

IV. 5D:[6]

Oh how is it that I could come out to here
And be still floating
And never hit bottom and keep falling through
Just relaxed and paying attention

All my two dimensional boundaries were gone
I had lost to them badly
I saw the world crumble and thought I was dead
But I found my senses still working

And as I continued to drop through the hole
I found all the surrounding
To show me the joy that innocently is
Just be quiet and feel it around you

And I opened my heart to the whole universe
And I found it was loving
And I saw the great blunder my teacher's had made
Scientific delirium madness

I will keep falling as long as I live
All without ending
And I will remember the place that is now
That has ended before the beginning

[6] Vgl. https://genius.com/The-byrds-5d-fifth-dimension-lyrics

Oh how is it that I could come out to here
And be still floating
And never hit bottom and keep falling through
Just relaxed and paying attention

V. What is the Fifth Dimension?:[7]

Much has been written, spoken and channeled about the Fifth Dimension and humanity's ascension into this new realm of existence.

In addition, many "ordinary" people are now having their own experiences, visions and inner "downloads" about the Fifth Dimension.

---

7 Vgl. http://vidyafrazier.com/what-is-the-fifth-dimension/#:~:text=The%20Fifth%20Dimension%20has%20been%20described%20as%20the,of%20separation.%20Mastery%20over%20thought%20is%20a%20prerequisite.

Not every source agrees on details about this dimensional reality, but most describe similar major characteristics, which are described below.

Ascension into the Fifth Dimension

According to ascension teachings, the earth and all beings living on the earth are in the process of shifting into a whole new level of reality in which a consciousness of love, compassion, peace and spiritual wisdom prevails. This has been called the Fifth Dimension.

Some say this shift will probably be complete within the next couple of decades; others give no date. But all seem to agree it will be complete sometime in the near future, although individuals will be each moving into the Fifth Dimension at their own rate when their frequency is high enough to match the vibration of the higher dimension.

Most teachings state that the shift the earth and humanity are taking into the Fifth Dimension has been "planned" for eons. Also that it has already been happening in the last few decades. December 21, 2012 was a date that was given as the mid-point of the shift taking place, and that it will continue to unfold in more and more obvious ways, picking up speed, as time goes on.

A Fairy Tale?

Much of what has been described about the Fifth Dimension can sound like a fairy tale:

- All people living in peace and harmony, experiencing oneness with all of life, fully respecting all people and the earth itself — love and compassion flowing through all communications
- Equality, justice and respect for all human beings reigning on earth—no more hunger, poverty or crime — abundance available to all

- Everyone living without fear—with complete trust in the Divine
- Everyone awake to the majestic, divine inter-dimensional beings they truly are

Some of the descriptions can sound even more "out there"—such as people freely communicating with beings from other planets and galaxies and traveling to distant parts of the universe with these beings.

Imagination, Memory or Intuition?

And yet, haven't we all had dreams of living in a world like this? Are these dreams just figments of our imagination?

Or are they memories of what we, thousands and thousands of years ago, once experienced—and at some point lost, as we descended into the kind of world we know of today, filled with struggle and suffering and lack of direct connection with the Divine?

Or do these dreams perhaps come from intuitions about the future that is in store for us? Many of us are having these intuitive feelings; some are having clear visions; others are inwardly hearing about the reality of humanity's future will be. Some of us feel we have been waiting thousands of years for these times we are now entering.

If we seek deeply within ourselves, we may find that these dreams of an ideal and peaceful world are actually both a distant memory of what we once experienced eons ago and an intuitive glimpse into what is now beginning to happen on earth.

And our longing to return to this ideal world is simply a yearning to finally return Home to this beautiful world ahead of us.

How Can it Happen so Quickly?

The question might arise: How can this possibly happen? How can this world turn around from where it is today and become this utopian kind of world? There is still so much darkness on the planet—wars, hatred, prejudice and injustice.

The answer is two-fold: First, thousands of people on the planet are now experiencing an awakening of the heart at an unprecedented rate—and this awakening appears to be speeding up, as time goes by. At some point, the hundredth monkey phenomenon will inevitably take hold.

And secondly, not everyone on the planet at this time is making the choice (consciously or unconsciously) to make the shift into the Fifth Dimension.

All souls have the choice to enter 5D, given they have assimilated sufficient light to hold the energy levels that exist in that higher vibration. But many will be choosing to leave the earth within the next couple of decades to move on to other third dimensional experiences in other parts of the universe. They will not have finished with what third-dimensional reality has still to teach them.

Those who are choosing to stay and make the shift with the earth will be going through some intense and rapid changes, as their bodies and minds make the radical changes needed to shift into the higher consciousness requisite for moving into the Fifth Dimension.

Exactly What are Dimensions?

First of all, dimensions are not places or locations; they're levels of consciousness that vibrate at a certain rate. There exist numerous dimensions; the fourth and fifth are simply higher than the one we've been living in. Ascension into even higher dimensions will continue even after we've reached the fifth.

Each dimension vibrates at a higher rate than the one below. In each higher dimension, there exists a clearer, wider perspective of reality, a greater level of knowing. We experience more freedom, greater power, and more opportunity to create reality.

In order for a higher dimension to be available to us, we need to vibrate in resonance with it. Shifting from one level of consciousness to the next higher one means becoming established on it, so we don't get pulled back.

The Third Dimension

It's important to understand, first off, that the Third Dimension is not the things you see: the table, the tree, the earth. These are form. All things in form are still present in the Fourth Dimension (and to some degree in the 5th); they're simply more light-filled, not as dense.

The Third Dimension is a state of consciousness that is very limited and restricted. Because we've been living in this 3rd dimensional reality for so many lifetimes, we tend to assume that this is the only reality available to live in. We think this is simply how "reality" is, not realizing it's a very limited experience of reality.

The Third Dimensional "operating system" runs on rigid beliefs and a fairly inflexible set of rules and limitations. For example, in the Third Dimension, we learn to believe that bodies are solid; they can't merge with each other or walk through walls. Everything is subject to gravity, physical objects cannot disappear, and we cannot read another person's mind. There's a solid belief in duality, and judgment and fear are pervasive.

The Fourth Dimension

This is the “bridge” we’re all pretty much on now, and will be for a relatively short period of time. In traveling through the Fourth Dimension, we are preparing ourselves for the Fifth.

Many of us have had experiences of the Fourth Dimension for a number of years now without realizing it.

We can know we're experiencing the Fourth Dimension when we have moments of spiritual awakening and experiences of heart opening. Other times, it can happen when we're simply feeling clear and quiet inside. Everything within and around us feels lighter, less rigid. There's a sense of spaciousness and upliftment.

Time is no longer linear in the Fourth Dimension—there's an ongoing sense of being in present time, with no interest or even awareness of past and future. And we can discover that time is malleable—it can actually stretch and condense, much to our third dimensional surprise.

Manifestation is much faster in the Fourth Dimension. Something we simply think about can show up very quickly. In general, when we're experiencing joy, love and gratitude, we're experiencing fourth dimensional consciousness.

The Fifth Dimension

The Fifth Dimension has been described as the dimension of Love, of living totally from the Heart.

In order to enter into the Fifth Dimension and stay there, all mental and emotional baggage must be left at the door. No fear, anger, hostility, guilt exists there—no suffering or sense of separation. Mastery over thought is a prerequisite.

Manifestation in the Fifth Dimension is instantaneous. You think about something—it comes present. People generally communicate through telepathy and have the ability to read each other's thoughts and feelings with ease. The experience of time is radically different:

some describe it as "everything happening at once." There is no distinction between past, present or future.

Many of us are having experiences (or "dreams") that feel like visits to the Fifth Dimension. These are exhilarating—tremendously exciting and hopeful. They keep us moving on through the difficulties that sometimes arise as we travel through the Fourth Dimension and into the Fifth.

Transitional Times

We are currently in what's been called "transitional times" or the "end times". These are the times in which we are experiencing the death of third-dimensional reality, while at the same time beginning to travel through new and unknown landscapes of the 4th Dimension.

In essence, one whole structure of reality is collapsing, while a new one is emerging. It's to be expected that some chaos, confusion and disorientation will reign both within and around us, as we attempt to adapt to a whole new way of experiencing reality.

Many of us are beginning to experience radical changes in our lives, as we enter into these times. Whatever does not serve us in shifting into a higher dimension has to fall away.

This can include old relationships, lifetime careers, approaches to life we've traditionally taken, an out-dated sense of identity, or any limited or negative thoughts and emotions that holds us in a lower vibration.

Fortunately, we can now get a great deal of help in making the transition to a higher vibration. Beings from higher dimensional realms are more and more present to assist us; we simply need to ask for their help.

We can also become aware of the flooding of divine light that's currently arriving from the higher dimensions. So releasing old patterns and negative emotions is getting easier and easier, if we have the clear intention of letting them go.

We Can take our Bodies with Us

Many sources tell us we can take our physical bodies with us, if we choose, into the Fifth Dimension.

Some say that although other planets and galaxies have shifted into higher dimensions before in the history of the universe, this is the first time that souls in incarnation on a planet are going to be taking their physical vehicles with them into the higher dimension. Doing this is seen as the next step in humanity's evolution.

Given this, it seems important for us to really take care of our bodies at this time. Radical transformation can be hard on the body, causing pain, aches, exhaustion and flu-like symptoms.

It's Up to You

If you feel a resonance with the information in this article, it's likely you've decided—either consciously or unconsciously—to shift with the earth into the Fifth Dimension in this lifetime. If so, you have the choice to simply allow life to transform you—sometimes in uncomfortable ways, if you have any resistance to change. Life will do the job for you.

Or you can choose to actively cooperate with the shifts taking place inside you. You can consciously let go of old patterns, release negative emotions, judgments and thoughts, and work on keeping your vibration high at all times. This effort will likely ensure that your journey through the Fourth Dimension will be a lot smoother and even perhaps more rapid.

But there's no right way to make this journey. We each have to do it the way that's best for us. One way or another, we will make it into the new reality that lies before us. What an exciting time to be alive!

Read more about the Fifth Dimension and your Ascension Journey

VI. Fifth Dimension:[8]

What is the Fifth Dimension

What is the Fifth Dimension? How can we awaken to this level of consciousness?

The 'Fifth Dimension' is a term often heard in spiritual and New Age circles. What does it really mean? Is there really something to it?

To help answer the question of what it really is, it is often best to ask to *feel* into it for yourself. This simple step of *asking* to feel

[8] Vgl. https://andreaoneness.com/fifth-dimension/

something is so helpful in accessing our own innate wisdom and knowledge.

Though basically, to answer the question of 'is there something to it?' or 'is the Fifth Dimension real?' – is Yes! there is something to it!

The Fifth Dimension is a Plane of Consciousness

The Fifth Dimension is a level of consciousness. We move into this level of consciousness after Self Realization has occurred.

I personally prefer to use the word 'level' or 'plane', rather than 'dimension' so that we don't overly give our power away to a big sounding word. But also because quite simply that is what it *feels* like, a plane. The Fifth Dimension feels like a vast plane that stretches out all around you.

Self Realization is the doorway into the Fifth plane of consciousness. The movement into the Fifth Dimension is another reason why Self Realization is so important.

The doorway itself is the Open Heart.

Self Realization is when a permanent opening in the heart forms. During Self Realization the 'I thought' dies, and an opening on the right side of the chest forms. Within this opening is a white lily.

The opening in the heart that forms during Self Realization is like a key, this key unlocks countless mysteries.

The Fifth Dimension Is Through Your Open Heart

Moving into the Fifth Dimension occurs some time after Self Realization. The heart must be open before we can move into the fifth dimension.

As is the case with all other spiritual awakening processes, these shifts occur when you are ready, and when you have removed old emotional densities and baggage.

What Occurs When We Enter The Fifth Dimension

The start of the process of entering into the Fifth Dimension is a sense of your viewpoint suddenly rotating within. Normally we have a sense of our inner point of view matching our vision. However all of a sudden there is a sense of your viewpoint rotating downwards, so that instead of looking straight in front of you, you are now looking straight down into the centre of the Earth. It is a strange and unsettling sensation, and there is a sense of simply being poised there, hovering. Once you are able to accept this shift in view point, there is then a strong sense of rushing downwards through this portal. Immediately there is then a sense of entering another plane. All of this is internal. Your physical body does not move or change in any way.

The plane that one enters is the Fifth Dimension.

When one first experiences this plane of consciousness it feels as though one is standing in the middle of the night sky. It is inky black, with softly glinting stars.

Stars, Planets, Beings of Light

All the stars, plants, nebulas, and universes upon universes are here, within your majestic heart.

As you start to take in this beautiful field of stars and planets that are here, within, there is simultaneously an awareness that there are also all these Beings here. Beings of Light. They are standing all around you, Celebrating You, Welcoming You. Celebrating your arrival into this plane of consciousness.

They are here ready, waiting, and willing to help you in any way that they are able. They have always been here, and always will be here, for You.

Overall, when one enters the Fifth Dimension there is a sense that one is not so anchored down into what feels like the ground, or earthly, plane. This perception of the ground is what we could call the 'Fourth Dimension'. The Fourth Dimension is what constitutes day to day awareness. After experiencing the Fifth Dimension, the Fourth feels dense, compacted, heavy and weighed down.

It is from the Fifth Dimension that the other levels of consciousness begin to open up and become more available for us. It is by journeying *through* the open heart, the incredible portal that it is, that we move into higher and more expansive states of Being.

All of these movements in consciousness take place naturally when old patterns, misunderstandings and general density leave us. There is nothing we need do other than give our soft attention to all the parts within that are calling for our presence. We do this by Processing Emotions.

We can access these Beings of Light and Love whenever we need to. Simply ask. We need never do anything alone.

The harder part is remembering to do so, and trusting that the Divine really is there for you. Something we all need reminding of no matter who we are and where we are at.

VII. Shifting Into The 5th Dimension:[9]

[9] Vgl. https://ledbysource.com/shifting-into-the-5th-dimension/

If you have been involved in the spiritual community for some time then chances are you have heard about a 5th dimensional shift that is occurring right now. It has been said that this period on Earth is a *time of awakening*.

This has been described as the splitting of two Earths – 3D and 5D for the creation of New Earth.

You might be wondering what the heck everyone is going on about? Will this be a physical shift? When exactly is this taking place? What does shifting to the 5th dimension look like?

There is such much unclear information out there and often we don't get a full picture of what living in these states actually looks like.

So in this article I wanted to clear up some of the common misconceptions around the 5th dimension and talk about my own experience of shifting into 5D and what it may look like for you.

What is 5D Consciousness?

Each dimension is a different level of consciousness that vibrates at a different rate. These are not physical locations but states of consciousness that we can tune into through our way of BEing.

Moving forward we are going to realize that these terms we use to describe different states of consciousness are only convenient labels, the reality is much more expansive and abstract than we can fathom now.

Each higher dimension opens you up to wider perspectives of reality. Despite the names there is no hierarchy between the different dimensions, each one simply has a different purpose in relation to your current work.

3D

This is the physical reality we chose to incarnate to and work through karma and the lessons this density provides. The physical realm is a great *training ground* for our consciousness, unlike 4D and 5D, 3D comes with immense suffering as well as incredible highs.

In 3D we work through problems by feeling through them, there is no other way. The density of 3D allows for heavy karma to be worked through and released. The suffering provides a contrast to pleasure allows us to navigate difficult lessons.

Many come to their spiritual awakening through the pain and suffering that we are able to experience in 3D, it works as a catalyst for your consciousness sparking the flame of awareness within you.

This 3D plane or Earth school is where we come to remember everything we have forgotten and tap back into our gifts and heal wounds from **past lives**.

While we are here it can feel like a hopeless place but once it is over we can appreciate the highs and the lows and how they helped work through the wounds that we hadn't healed. It's for this reason that we ultimately chose to incarnate back here time and time again, coming back for further missions.

4D

We hear a lot about 3D and 5D but often 4D is left out of it completely! I like to think of 4D as **the bridge between the two**, so having a way to discern if you are already there is a good way to progress further. So what does a shift to 4D consciousness look like?

4th dimension consciousness is where we no longer perceive reality in a strictly linear fashion, our concept of time and space expands. 4D consciousness is what we start shifting into when we apply the Law of Attraction popularized by the book *The Secret*.

Learning to bend time and space to bring forth our manifestations to reality. You don't simply follow reality but reality starts to curve around your emotions and intentions. It can fee as if events are being narrated to us before they occur.

Our waking lives feel like a dream state and our dreams become incredibly vivid. We experience constant synchronicity. When you focus on something it manifests to you incredibly fast. The boundaries that separate you and other beings dissolve.

Most people going through the beginning stages of a spiritual awakening will be familiar with the 4th dimension. It feels like having one foot in the physical world and another in the spiritual world.

You're experiencing an energetic shift but also the physical symptoms associated with this. You go through mood swings, tiredness, headaches, tummy aches and you may experience **ringing in the ears**. These symptoms are making way for a new way of being, clearing up the energetic density in your body.

5D

Originally there was a lot of information depicting a 5th dimensional shift as a kind of physical exodus, some people would attain 5D consciousness and leave behind those that did not.

It was a very 'us vs them' mentality. However we are now moving into the knowing that 5D is less about the physical (although physical changes will come as a result too) and more about the work we are doing from the inside out to embody our highest selves and connect with Source.

A 5D consciousness shift has nothing to do with physical location, it is about **being all here right now**. It's about dropping into your heart center and seeing all as one. It is a state of oneness with all. You no longer reach for more because it is all here in this moment, the eternal NOW.

5D is all about choosing how you want to BE in this moment. Embodying your highest self in every moment, reintegrating your highest self and remembering what you have forgotten.

What Does a 5th Dimension Shift Look Like?

Now you might be wondering what living in 5D looks like? How exactly does one balance these higher dimensions with day to day Earthly duties?

We are constantly dipping in and out of these states as we go about our day. Sometimes we might be more focused on the physical, other times we might be focused on manifestation and living in a more dreamlike state, and other times we are completely submerged in the moment.

It's not that we *have* to live in 5D every moment of everyday but that we should aim to bring some of this consciousness into our everyday lives. Spending time each day where our main focus is the present moment.

A 5D shift looks like striking a delicate balance between tending to your physical duties and finding peace in each moment.

5D Living

When I started **meditating** everyday and bringing that state into day to day life instead of confining it to the ten to twenty minutes, the world around me started o change.

It was as if I was walking in a dream, there was a **lucidity in waking life** that I had never experienced before. I saw synchronicity as I usually did but in breathtaking fashion. I could pick up on other people's emotions and thoughts as if they were talking to me telepathically.

I would walk around and have an inner commentary narrating things before they happened. I knew I had shifted but it also appeared as if other people were shifting too. Everyone around me seemed unusually upbeat.

Experiencing these moments of lucidity as you go about your day completely changes how you view the world, as you can viscerally feel and ***see*** moment to moment how your inner world creates your outer one.

Bring awareness to each moment. In the way you eat, sleep, work and interact with others. Be mindful in how you respond to external situations and inner conflicts. This is the process of healing and releasing. Inject consciousness into more and more moments.

NOW you have the choice of where to put your awareness. Right now you have the choice to begin shifting into a new way of being. You are gradually sinking deeper and deeper into this highest version of your self and fully embodying it while still here on physical Earth.

VIII. Ascending Into The 5th Dimension:[10]

Consciously Choosing to Shift Into 5D

The shift of consciousness into the 5th dimension is underway and it has been for some time. Many of the changes of this shift have gone unseen, and yet this shift is very real.

The shift into the 5th dimension is happening and it is being subtly carried forward with guidance from the realms of spirit, and through the conscious choice and action from countless individuals.

As time continues to accelerate, so too does the shifting of consciousness.

---

10 Vgl. https://www.ask-angels.com/spiritual-guidance/ascending-into-the-5th-dimension/

So what does a shift in consciousness look like? How is this all unfolding in reality and where is the proof that this great spiritual shift is actually happening?

To answer these questions. Let's first look at consciousness in a metaphorical sense. One of the most accurate ways I have heard human consciousness described is as a complex tapestry.

The vast and intricate tapestry of human consciousness contains all of the thoughts, qualities, beliefs and experiences of individual humans.

The experiences, beliefs, and choices of individuals as well as groups, are woven together in a divinely designed pattern, which is the fabric of consciousness.

Although we may still at times perceive ourselves as separate individuals, through the tapestry of consciousness we are united... We exist within one fabric of creation, and together we are shifting.

Through individual choice, the very threads within the fabric of consciousness are changing. As a result, the entire tapestry will change.

Consciousness is changing, and in many senses, it has already changed.

In this shift into the 5th dimension, some threads within the fabric of consciousness will be removed completely, some are being transformed, others elevated in their vibration. Some of the threads are completely altered in their texture, form, and frequency. This is also known as ascension.

Through ascension, one thread at a time, the entire tapestry of consciousness is being elevated.

One thread at a time, or in other words one choice at a time, one moment, and one person at a time, the great shift of the ages and the progression into living in the 5th dimension is happening.

Consciousness is shifting by raising the entire tapestry of consciousness in vibration.

Already the fabric of consciousness has changed significantly... There are threads within the fabric that are no longer in place as individuals have let go of old habits and beliefs they once held.

There are also many dense emotions, fears, and perceptions which were commonly experienced in the 3rd and 4th dimensions which simply do not exist in the higher vibrations of the 5th dimension. These dense energies, emotions, and experiences have no place in the tapestry of higher consciousness and so they are coming up for review, and for release before being completely replaced, transformed, or released.

To facilitate the divine shift of ascension, the consciousness of your higher self in spirit guides you. Are you listening?

This process for releasing the old and outdated is not automatic. However, it is Divinely guided, and yet in the moment when dense emotion arises, each individual has the choice to cling to the old, or to meet the dense thread of thought, belief or emotion with compassion, awareness, and with the willingness to let it go.

One moment and one person at a time, a vibrational change to the tapestry of consciousness is happening.

Much of what is occurring in this great shift has yet to be observed by the masses. Many people do not realize the changes are already happening beneath the surface. They don't realize the huge control they have now in regards to creating the future they will live in.

It's no surprise. The old paradigm of living life in a reactionary sense was built on a foundation of illusion. There are many distractions, and layers of belief, and deception that hide the underlying truth from the masses.

The truth is that this shift into 5D is ours to create.

Indeed the shift into the 5th dimension is happening and as it does, old patterns, and threads within the tapestry which make up the old foundation will be dissolved. As a result, things may seem a bit chaotic.

This is part of the shift and sometimes the only way for the old threads of thoughts, beliefs and habits to fall away is for them to crumble.

The Earth is shifting, too. You can see this present in changes in weather, increased solar activity of the sun, increasing numbers of earthquakes and volcanic eruptions... These are all perceivable evidence that the Earth is quite literally shifting.

Many of the threads of consciousness contained within the third (*phsyical*) and fourth (*astral and imaginary*) dimensional experience cannot exist in the higher vibrations of the 5th Dimension. Co-creation, love, beauty, collaboration and well-being create the new foundation of consciousness in the 5th dimension.

Guided by your higher self, your angels, guides, and by the Divine, you are able to step into the new paradigm now.

The choice belongs to each of us now. It's not a choice to make once though, it's a choice to return to time and time again in every moment.

Are you willing to let go of the old patterns that no longer serve? Are you willing to let go of what is familiar and known to us, so you can step into new opportunity?

Do you choose to hold on to the uncomfortable aspects of the third and fourth dimension of experience you are accustomed to because it feels safe and secure and because it is what has always been?

Or are you willing to choose the new?

Are you willing to follow the guidance of your Higher Self, your guides, angels and to co-create with the light of the Divine that continues to stream onto the planet?

Are you willing to bring the truth of your spiritual nature into your reality?

The old tapestry is no more.

The consciousness of the higher dimensions is already here and the foundation of reality has already shifted.

There is no going back to what was… So the question is, are you willing to move forward?

Are you willing to be an active participant in the new consciousness and the new earth?

New opportunities and choices will continue to emerge for all of us who do make this choice. New possibilities to co-create and collaborate will appear.

Collectively we are at a crossroads. Do we sit back and wait to react to the changes this will bring? Or do we choose to re-create our collective tapestry with new threads of beauty, love, well-being, and joy to replace those old threads which are already gone?

The choice is present in this moment… Enter into the new paradigm through love. It is here and it is up to us to create this new reality, together.

The entrance into the 5th dimension, otherwise known as the golden age, is clearly happening and the outer manifestation of this will continue to become more apparent to the masses and you have the opportunity to be a way-shower.

One step at a time, one moment at a time and one person at a time we are able to boldly create the new world in the 5th dimension, in alignment with love.

IX. Is Earth Moving into the 4th or 5th Dimension in this year of COVID-19?:[11]

Yep, 2020 is the year! — or maybe it will be 2034?

For the past decade, at least, New Age spiritualists and channeled beings have been talking about how the planet Earth is transitioning or ascending from the 3rd Dimension to the 4th or 5th Dimension. It was as if each year was "the year" that this ascension was supposed to happen. But the "New Earth" that was envisioned never quite materialized as was predicted — or at least it was hard to see.

This year, however, the dramatic worldwide impact of the COVID-19 pandemic has increased some people conviction that such a

[11] Vgl. https://medium.com/new-earth-consciousness/is-earth-moving-into-the-4th-or-5th-dimension-in-this-year-of-covid-19-71728dcbe39d

transition is taking place now more than in any year before. Maybe they are right.

Some still hold to the belief, more common in the past, that the Earth will shift suddenly and completely from being a 3rd Dimensional planet to being a 4th or 5th Dimension one. Those with this type of expectation are usually disappointed.

Photo by United Nations COVID-19 Response on Unsplash

Others frame it in a more nuanced manner by emphasizing that we 3rd Dimensional Earth humans are learning, using, and applying more and more 4th and 5th dimensional skills and perceptions in our lives. Eventually (maybe on Dec. 21, 2020?), a tipping point will be reached in which these skills are considered “normal”.

4th Dimensional consciousness skills include: using our intuition and creativity; practicing forms of meditation and yoga; learning lucid dreaming and out-of-body experience (OBE) techniques; channeling and otherwise communicating with higher dimensional beings and ETs; and working with past life regression, hypnosis, and psychic abilities. These modalities both bring the practitioner into the 4th and higher dimension, and bring those dimensions into the 3rd Dimension.

WHAT ARE SPIRITUAL DIMENSIONS?

In comparison to our 3rd Dimension Earth, most higher dimensions are characterized as having less stress and suffering, more harmony and cooperation, less egocentric behavior and exploitation, more wisdom and understanding, less separation and “*othering*”, and more oneness and love.

Detailed definitions of the different spiritual dimensions vary, but are similar at general levels. One approach associates the dimensions with the 7 chakras. Our 3rd Dimensional Earth is one where the 3rd Chakra (Solar Plexus) is dominant in the consciousness of most humans. This makes sense, as the 3rd Chakra emphasizes personal power, individualism, and control. A 4th Dimensional Earth would find most humans having a 4th Chakra (Heart) consciousness, which is based in love, harmony, and spiritual and psychic connections.

The reason the 5th Dimension comes up is because some writings characterize the 4th Dimension as a realm of lower vibration astral beings (sort of like a nightmare with monsters). The 5th Dimension has higher vibrational beings who operate from unconditional love and oneness, which is often likened to 'Heaven on Earth', or a lucid dream in which you have complete control to create anything you want.

Following this understanding, we would want to carefully bypass the 4th Dimension and move directly to the 5th by developing our heart-based love energy. However, other see the 4th Dimension as being much broader than this narrow definition, as this is where we will meet and work closely with beings from other planets in our galaxy and beyond.

(For a more detailed look at the spiritual dimensions, see my article: Explainer: Just What are the Different Spiritual Dimensions of Reality?)

WHAT IS THE ASCENSION?

The 'transition' or 'ascension' (both terms are widely used) to the 4th/5th Dimension may have started at the end of World War II, with the invention and use of the atomic bomb. Higher dimensional beings (including extra-terrestrials, spiritual guides, angels, and others) started to take much more interest in our planet at that time and have been working to prevent us from destroying ourselves ever since.

source: https://pixabay.com/photos/ascension-celestial-planet-heaven-1568162/

Some point to the music and protest movements of the 1960s (the "Love Revolution") as the start of the planet's transition to a higher dimension. Astrologically, it is seen as the transition from Age of Pisces, which started about 2000 years ago, to the Age of Aquarius (which some say officially started in July 2020). This transition was highlighted in the song *Aquarius* from the 1967 musical, *Hair*, and made famous by The 5th Dimension in 1969 when their version was at the top of the pop music charts.

The end of the Mayan Calendar, on December 21, 2012, is also pointed to as a milestone of the planet's ascension out of the denser 3rd Dimension. Evidence of the transformation in recent decades is seen in the tremendous growth around the world in yoga, meditation, wellness and alternative healing arts, spiritual teachers, and channeling and communicating with spirit guides and ETs (also known as “galactics”). Much of the explosion in these areas has been enhances by the globalization of the internet.

For example, much of the information is this article is based on messages from different higher dimensional channeled beings communicating through different human channelers, and shared on YouTube. That practice alone has become “normal” and commonplace to a degree unthinkable a decade of two ago.

Some of these beings say that our present shift to a higher dimension was a decision made by Mother Earth (or ‘Gaia’), after experimenting with the lower 3rd Dimension for many thousands of years. From this perspective, we humans (along with plants and animals) are being pulled into the 4th/5th Dimension by the planet. (Some say the Sun is also helping with this.) We have no choice—and, in fact most are totally unaware that this is happening to them.

Other say that the universe and everything in it is always ascending, and again, we really don’t have a lot of say in the matter. On the other hand, those of us alive today chose to be born at this time specifically to experience and help with this particular transition. Others are using the COVID-19 pandemic to leave the planet at this time because they had no intention to experience a 4th Dimension Earth in this incarnation.

Some say the people on Earth have mostly had a 3rd Dimensional consciousness for the past 5 to 10 thousand years (since the Bronze Age). Throughout that time, however, there have always been some people who had developed 4th, 5th and higher dimensional states of consciousness, such as saints, seers, mystics, and spiritual teachers in many different belief systems.

https://pixabay.com/illustrations/hands-globe-earth-protection-1222866/

The coming transition is basically being driven by a significant rise at this time in the number of people on the planet who have developed their 4th/5th dimensional consciousness. Again, I think the Internet has helped with this.

If you are simply aware that, at some level within you, you have psychic abilities, whether or not you intentionally ever use them, then I welcome you to the 4th Dimension.

Others, however, do not see the transition being fully realized until 2029, the 2030s, or 2040s, in 100 years, and in 1,000 years. In general, by late 2020, it seems that channelers are more likely to be talking about a gradual transition over at least a decade than in the next year.

Another perspective sees the 3rd Dimension as when most humans identified solely with their physical body and were asleep to their spiritual being. The 4th Dimension was when most woke up to identify with their spiritual consciousness (or soul), beyond their physical body.

In the 4th Dimension we are essentially learning to communicate with our Higher Self. The Higher Self is sometimes defined as the aspect of us that is at the highest individuated level, closest to the universal mind or soul. Other times, it is mores simply any aspect of ourselves that is in a higher dimension that we are most of the time.

The 5th Dimension is reached when humans start to create their physical reality from their larger consciousness, like a god (small "g"). Based on this approach, some say we are already in the 5th Dimension because there are so many people today who are experiencing and mastering this higher state of awareness and consciousness in their lives.

Their higher vibration is infectious and is changing the world around them. Some say we only need 144,000 people on the planet who can do this to shift the entire Earth to a higher dimension (which is a

New Age spiritualist interpretation of that number from the Bible). Others say it will take 1%, 2% or 3% if the Earth's human population (2% would be 156 million people).

A few see humanity splitting, with some staying on this 3rd Dimensional version of Earth, while others physically move to a new 5th Dimensional version of the planet. They say that this New Earth is hidden from our current view on the opposite side of the Sun. (To me, this is the least convincing understanding.)

Most say that at some point, which is difficult to predict, we will be re-connected with intelligent beings on the other planets in our solar system and galaxy who mostly communicate and travel using 4th and higher dimensional technologies. This connection existed on our planet in the past, but was lost when Mother Earth decided to try her 3rd Dimensional experiment.

HOW WILL WE ASCEND?

The tensions, confusion and fear felt by many on Earth in 2020 have been described as similar to "culture shock" caused by the expansion of lighter dimensional energies (cultures) that are pushing people into new mental territory. Some channelers say that COVID-19 is bringing every person on the planet into a new relationship with their self — away from a physical mind-body dominance (3rd Dimension) to a more spiritual-heart dominance (4th/5th Dimension).

Most of these "new culture" changes are subtle and do not make the nightly news cycle. On the other hand, those who are resisting these changes and trying to stay in a lower 3rd Dimensional vibration are much more likely to make the headlines.

As the Earth is expanding to a higher dimension, so is the entire universe, on all dimensions, transitioning to a lighter density. This, is being felt in similar ways by beings in all dimensions — so we are not alone. Also, all entities on the planet Earth are ascending, including animals, plants, and inanimate objects, like computers and cars — at least this is what some suggest is happening.

People and beings who generate positive energies, based in love, will manage the ascension much better than those who resist. Such people / beings are needed at all dimensional levels of reality (not just Earth) at this time to make the ascension for the universe as smooth as possible. In addition, the more successful we can make this transition on Earth, the more we will be helping the entire universe.

source: https://pixabay.com/photos/fantasy-mystical-stargate-planet-4932109/

Some channeled beings say that the model for a New Earth is based on what has been developed on planets around the star Sirius. Sirian human-like races have 3rd Dimension physical bodies, but travel and communicate across the galaxy using 4th and 5th Dimensional technologies. Other say that it is the Arcturians who are the model for a 5th Dimensional Earth.

I have also heard that Pleaidians are from the 5th Dimension, Sirians are from the 6th Dimension, and Artcurians are from the 7th Dimension. This comes from a 15 dimension model of existence.

Ascension Means Integration

The expansion of 4th Dimensional technologies and skills on Earth is the main way that the transformation of our 3rd Dimension is taking place. There are the two basic ways that this is done: (1) bringing the 4th Dimension into the 3rd, such as when using intuition or channeling one's higher self to solve a problem; and (2) leaving the 3rd Dimension to experience the 4th, such as in a lucid dream.

The more we accept and normalize the use of 4th Dimensional modalities, especially those with a focus on the Heart Chakra, the more the planet will reflect a higher and lighter dimensional vibration.

The COVID-19 pandemic has accelerated Earth's movement beyond a 3rd Dimensional consciousness (or mindset) and into a 4th Dimensional one. It is showing us what we dislike about the 3rd Dimension (such as excessive rules, restrictions, fear, and separation), and what we truly value in our lives: freedom, fresh air, nature, companionship, community, and love — all of which are Heart Chakra values.

In the short term (the next one to ten years), this is what I see:

(1) 4th and 5th Dimensional **technologies** will rapidly develop and become commonplace, including energy healing, new sources of almost free electricity, and new forms of interplanetary and dream travel; dreams will be more lucid and remembered by everyone and group dreaming will be more common; time travel is probably a bit further away; **science** and **medicine** will evolve new dominant paradigms that merge objective and subjective realities (this is already starting to happen); both will become quantum-based and medicine, in particular, will become individualized, with treatments tailored to the unique conditions of each person.

(2) 4th and 5th Dimensional thinking will expand and eventually become common, including awareness of universal **oneness** and respect for human **diversity** and our natural environments, along with greater international **cooperation** to end wars, conflicts and poverty; as a result of these shifts, locally oriented **economic systems** will expand as global economies become less pronounced; and new forms of **government** will emerge to reflect these new values, perhaps similar to more idealistic and compassionate forms of libertarian thought.

(3) Communication with 4th and 5th Dimensional beings (ETs/galactics, spirit guides, etc.) will become more common as **intuitive** communication skills (including telepathy) and **inner**

spirituality develop; **religions**, and moral behavior in general, will be completely redefined because of this shift, with both becoming more tolerant and even encouraging a wider and more colorful range of "normal" human behavior and beliefs.

(4) Along with enhanced and alternate ways of communicating, individual humans will increasingly exhibit a wider range of **psychic skills**, including knowledge from their Higher Self, which will be considered normal (this is already starting to happen); such skills will be widely taught from elementary schools through universities, and **education** will change in major ways because of this, toward more cooperative learning rather than top-down teaching.

This is how I understand the planet's ascension taking place, based on the diverse and sometimes conflicting messages I have heard from channeled higher dimensional beings.

KEEP CALM AND ENJOY THE RIDE

The 3rd Dimensional physical Earth is not going anywhere, and is not going to flip suddenly into a different dimension. Instead, it is integrating with the 4th and 5th dimensions. That is what the ascension or transformation is all about. I think having a more heart-centered planet can only be a good thing.

We still have a ways to go, however, with many shadows that need to be worked out across the globe. We will see resistance to this change, especially in the short term (the next five years). And even once we reach a planet-wide, mostly 4th Dimensional consciousness, it will probably take awhile longer to get to a 5th Dimensional "Heaven on Earth".

By being open to open to alternative realities and focusing on developing our 4th Dimensional consciousness, and with support from our 4th Dimensional extra-terrestrial allies and the Planet Earth itself, this vision can become a living realization.

Some channelers say that we Earth humans are among of the most powerful beings in the universe — much more so than any ET or archangel. We truly can create our own reality. We just need to awaken to this knowledge, and that is the direction we are all moving towards. So love your life and enjoy the ride.

ADDENDUM

ASCENSION OF CONSCIOUSNESS

3D → 4D → 5D

3D

Ego association
Service to self
Duality
Polarization
Labels
Separatism
Control
Rules
Status
Materialism
Hard working
Linear thinking
Fear-lower emotions-fear-based programming
Cause and effect
Linear thinking
Victim mentality
Dense-slow-heavy

4D

Mixed state-gateway
Conscious being
Expanding consciusness
Challenging old belief system
Comparison-duality still
Seeking answers
Understanding structures
Awareness of connection
More compassion
Aligning with purpose
Remembering
Synchronicity
Flexible reality
Faster manifestation
More connected

5D

Unity consciousness
Aligning with the divine
Heart-centered
Service to others
Purpose based
Connectedness
High frequencies
Authenticity
Activated senses
Flow-state
Abundance
Source information
Unconditional sharing
Guided, supported
Co-creator
Effortless, light, ease
Universal knowledge

facebook_1602563635356_6721639066032095466

Added Oct 13, 2020: I have seen various versions of this table posted recently on Facebook. It is, of course, one definition of 3D/4D/5D, but it comes fairly close to my own view at this time.

My main issue with this chart is the "heaven on Earth" image of 5D — which is a very common view. However, all dimensions have their challenges.

My guess is that the challenge of 5D is to ascend from a physical body to a non-physical body. There are probably others. However, I have seen people on Facebook claim that we will still have physical bodies in 6D and beyond.

In addition, this chart seems to only focus on humans. If the whole planet and universe are ascending, then would these same concepts apply to plants, animals, planets, and stars?

NOTES

Influences: I have been a follower of the teachings of the channeled being, Seth (Jane Roberts), for a good portion of my life. More recently I have been listening to many other channeled beings introduced by Kevin Moore in his "They Call Us Channelers" YouTube docuseries. What I present above is distilled from my many notes trying to figure out the different dimensions from these sources. I also channel my own Energy Group, which have influenced this article. The Chakra references are based on the teachings of the channeler Lincoln Gergar. My favorite source of 4th Dimensional insights is the channeling by Ivan Teller.

Printed by Books on Demand GmbH, Norderstedt / Germany